MOTHER'S KITCHEN AND OTHER PLACES

Poetry

ANTREKA M. TLADI

Mwanaka Media and Publishing Pvt Ltd,
Chitungwiza Zimbabwe
*
Creativity, Wisdom and Beauty

Publisher: *Mmap*
Mwanaka Media and Publishing Pvt Ltd
24 Svosve Road, Zengeza 1
Chitungwiza Zimbabwe
mwanaka@yahoo.com
mwanaka13@gmail.com
https://www.mmapublishing.org
www.africanbookscollective.com/publishers/mwanaka-media-and-publishing
https://facebook.com/MwanakaMediaAndPublishing/

Distributed in and outside N. America by African Books Collective
orders@africanbookscollective.com
www.africanbookscollective.com

ISBN: 978-1-77933-168-7
EAN: 9781779331687

© Antreka M. Tladi 2023

All rights reserved.
No part of this book may be reproduced or transmitted in any form or by any means, mechanical or electronic, including photocopying and recording, or be stored in any information storage or retrieval system, without written permission from the publisher

DISCLAIMER
All views expressed in this publication are those of the author and do not necessarily reflect the views of *Mmap*.

TABLE OF CONTENTS

Mother's Kitchen
The Red Dress
Motherhood
Life is a Train
Iron Fists
Flavoured
Fatherless
Missing Stars
Watching from Above
Remembering Home
Fetching for water
Visitors
My Shanty Shack
Cries of Unborn Children
Not a Night of Sleep
AZANIA, the fading Rainbow
African Baobabs
The Drunkard
House Chores
Laughter and Cries
Cleaning Services
The First Raindrop
Where do you come From
Mob Justice
The Demonstrators
My Midnight Star
Home Sparrows

Death
Household Accountant
Smoking Guns
Painting
When it's Dark
Listening to music
The black Crow
Conquering Fear
Rain
Whirlwinds of Freedom
THABANG (REJOICE)
Lost In Love
Your Touch
Searching for Love?
I'm Human
Who Are We?
Home, A Battlefield
Behind Closed Doors
A Home of Storms
Love Will Find You
I'm the Colour of the Night
A beautiful sight
Dust to Dust
The Naked Night Of The City
Home Is A Box
Hide and Seek
The Wardrobe
The Curfew
Sky Blue
0091Train To Mamelodi

The Calling
Afloat
Tears Fall Away from home
The Entire Lifetime Of A Poem
Red Sunset
Would You Love Me
Moon Watch
It Will Be Okay
A Bright Face, A Guiding Light
Down and Out
Clenching Of Jaws
I wish I'd Said
Slain
Wayfinding
Born In Chaos
The Christmas Of Old

Acknowledgements

I have had a number of poems in this collection published in various anthologies and journals,

This is my first collection of poems.

"Mother's kitchen " is published on Avbob poetry project library.

"fetching for water" was a third finalist for Avbob mini poetry competition

On world water day 2023.

"Dust to Dust " is published in an Anthology (Songs of the wind) in Uganda.

"Cries of the unborn children, Not a Night of Sleep and Azania, the Fading Rainbow" are published in Speaking Truth to Power Anthology (IHRA) curated by Uche Akunebu in Nigeria.

"Watching from Above and Missing Stars" are translated into Spanish and published in an Anthology (Sensei.com, Poets of the world) in Ecuador and also on Fundza literary Trust.

"The first Raindrop " is published in an anthology (Earth Poetree Collection 2022) and has been honoured by an African Honoree Authors' Award 2022.

"Life is a train, Motherhood, My midnight star, When it's dark, Painting " have been published on Fundza literary trust and also on my Facebook poetry page.

"Iron Fists, Flavoured and Cleaning Services "are published in the Otherwise Engaged Literature

And Art journal from New Mexico, USA.

"Household Accountant, Laughter and Cries, House Chores" are published in Writing Women Anthology

Published Zimbabwe by Mwanaka Media and publishing.

"Lost In love" is published in Cupid's Arrow curated by Abigirl Phiri in Zimbabwe.

"A Home of Storms "is published in the calabash literary journal (vol. 6) in RSA.

"Tears fall away from home" is published in the international human rights art movement

Preface

Mother's kitchen and other places is a collection of poems reflecting on life's memorable moments from growing up in the intertwining entanglements of life in South Africa to a contemplation of emotions in love, memories, hardships of domestic violence and grief. It magnifies ordinary day to day trivial moments; captured in words and seek hope in elements of nature as the human life journeys through the human condition in search of purpose.

Mother's Kitchen

In the aroma of Sunday-made curries,

The lemon sprinkled cakes,

Memorable moments find life again

And drift on the breeze.

Beyond and below my eyes

I see the layout of a table,

A kitchen taking the shape of a heart

And its body a fusion of spices.

Daily dishes still cook themselves

In remembrance of your warmth;

I would have chopped the onions if I could

But tears have depleted my strength.

I can't get used to the empty chair

Across the table, the unfolded napkins;

Unforgettable, a hand

That once cooked with these pots.

The Red Dress

Days after you were gone,
I couldn't bear the thought of
Giving away your dress, the red one.

So there, it hangs after all,
On a rusty steel hanger
Upon the bedroom wall.

I would sit and watch it for days
Thinking of the day you came into my life
Like unfolding petals to sunrays.

Then the perfume faded
As it hang there odourless and empty,
Invisible, silent and jaded.

Yesterday Sarah came out like a mistress
Stunning on her twenty first birthday

Rocking in your red dress.

Motherhood

The child was left crying;
On his own and uncared for,
Mother danced nights away
With loveless men.

Drinking might push
Days down the canals
Of the years
And when mother returns
The child is a man,

She realise she can't
Go on drinking no more
And struggle to understand
The man who's not a child anymore.

Life is a Train

Grandmama said;
Child, you should wake before sunrise
Never get late to school
And show love to all mankind.

Grandmama said;
Be thoughtful and considerate,
Console those in distress
Yet be careful who you trust.

Grandmama said;
Love and uplift your family
Because when I'm gone
You'll be all alone my child.

Standing beside her grave today,
I remember her lessons
And know that her train is on its way home,

As I wait for the next train

To bring me home too.

Iron Fists

After she has given taste to a man's lust,
After she has given colour to his bed,
Like the salt or the flowers of this earth
She'll be kept in a glass jar,
Disposable after use.

But first she'll be deprived of water
Until she's wilted and worn,
Then her body will become a battlefield;
Her face,
Blue eyed and bloodshot
Would learn to soak up
Iron fists,
Boot kicks
And bullet holes.

Like a punching bag
She would swing back and forth

Against kitchen and bathroom walls

That have become so cold and so quiet,

Where her orphaned children

Still roam the dusty and dirty floors

Last swept by their mama's hand,

With tears in their eyes.

Flavoured

Back then in my time,

Black education didn't fit

In a leather made backpack,

Instead I carried it

In an empty Tastic rice bag

Or a yellow Shoprite shoppers bag.

I brought firewood to school

From my mama's thatched hut

To cook it up like bones,

All three hours sizzling and boiling

In a black three foot pot

Upon a blazing fire,

Before it would be stuffed in my mouth.

I hanged an enamel mug

Upon the lapels of my khakhi shorts

Just in case it came as liquid

So that it may be poured down my throat,

Chill cold and sugarless.

But it was in that tasteless pouring,

Stuffing and feeding

That I learnt to turn myself into flavour,

For a nation that tasted of oppression and injustice.

Fatherless

Through hurdles and hardship
I saw myself grow up
Without a father,
Raised by the streets devoid of kindness,
Of care and paternal love.

I felt abandoned,
I felt neglected,
Then every stranger's face
Became my father's face.

I raised a child
Within the walls of my heart
Who learnt to become a father
To every child lost
To the misery of the streets.

It is true;

That an orphaned child

Is raised by the hearts

Of strangers.

Missing Stars

Sorrow would teach you
To gather everything you have
And guard it well.

I have seen how days come as thieves,
Searching and probing my heart
Of what little hope is left.

Every yesterday has taken a part of me away,
I've lost years in that way unaware.

I've lost stars in the skies of my nights,
Bright faces that guided me
When I was astray,
Voices that cheered me up and held me upright
When nights were long
And mornings delayed their arrival.

Yet some days

Came not as thieves but as a reminder

To cherish and rejoice for this moment.

Watching From Above

She watched from above
The misspelled epitaph
Upon the gravestone of her grave.

They wrote her down
As the girl who went away
Before her accepted time,
So young and full of hope,
So bright her future seemed,
Yet she left children alone
In the harsh silence of a world
Without care and tenderness.

A world that raises its children
By marching them in the cold,
Ignorant of their cries
Like sheep in the field
Bleating and protesting in silence.

She watched from above

As they are taught to remember

Her face upon torn photographs that;

Despite their faded texture still managed to solicit

One or two expensive smiles.

Remembering Home

I remember an ancient song,

Sung by tongues only understood

By dancers with feet caressing and massaging

The scar whipped spines of Africa's crouching back.

Bowed and bleeding,

The drums sounded and echoed

Alongside redbuck horns

Calling us again back home

To listen to the earth singing.

Uncut; the intertwining umbilicals

Twist and weave a tapestry of cultures,

A singular cry from Cape to Cairo

That spreads like the baobabs roots

Beside streams and lakes

That run uphill with humility.

Out of the fertile ground of hate

We grew tall as the trees

And embraced each other high up in the sky,

So that those

Beneath

Our shade, my feel our love

And treat our roots with compassion.

The flowers that grew in the desert

Became a city, a paradise on the banks of Nile,

Where the sun rise with the spirit of Ubuntu

To course its way from Addis to Lagos,

Amidst the shade of these trees

And sounds of the drums;

Nubia bred us and we became children of the song.

I remember an ancient song

That is beaten from the oxen hide,

That is blown out of redbuck horns

And it reminds me of home.

Fetching For Water

Everyday after school I come home

Drained, dirty and dusty,

Mother scold me

And send me down the spring

To fetch for water.

I shove and push the old rusty wheelbarrow

And race it through the dry Savanna

To fetch for mama's water.

The empty canisters jump and bounce

In the wheelbarrow, sounding like a coming thunder

In a country ravaged by droughts

Where thunderstorms are hard to come by.

Then kneeling down beside the spring

Like an alchemist to the sacredness of water,

I scooped the water in a gourd-

Patiently, with steady a hand
And filled the plastic canisters.

Filled them with water for mama's cooking,
Filled them with water for mama's washing,
Filled them with water for mama's cleaning,
Filled them with water for our drinking
For Water is life.

Visitors

At last the visitors;

Had gathered their memories

With all their belongings

And other emergency essentials

In a wheeled luggage and had gone.

The mood in the village;

Turns slowly

To the accustomed monotony of days that are;

Too long to do anything,

Too hot to go anywhere,

But sit still beneath the shade

Of an avocado tree

And watch the empty heavens.

Now the streets are silent and deserted,

Except the occasional cockerel crowing

And another one in the distance,

The song of the sparrows upon the mango trees.

Now you can hear clearly;

The rumbling of an airplane overhead

Lazily crossing the rural sky

Carrying more visitors back across the oceans.

My Shanty Shack

My shack is a house with one door
Has rats crawling upon the floor.

It's a kitchen, living and bed room all in one
My girlfriend doesn't like it and I stay alone.

When rainy water pours in everywhere
And drench the blankets I wear.

It looks like the house of the dead
But at least it's a roof over my head.

When stormy it is thrown all around
A little prayer keeps it on the ground.

My shack is a house with one window
That cast me a terrifying shadow.

Oh God! I'm tired of this shack of tricks

I want to build a house of bricks.

The Cries of Unborn Children

I see it in their mother's eyes,
Her ocean deep dark eyes
That have seen all evil until
They ran out of tears.

I hear the silent cry of unborn children,
Crying for a home they'll never have,
Crying for a bright sunny day
That will never come.

They're crying for a future that will never be,
For a continent that dances
To a tune of gunshots,
They cry for their father's land
And the echoing chorus of wailing and lamentations
Is heard across all the African diaspora.

They cry for their mother who carry

Bundles upon their filial necks,

Quarrelling their way across borders

With all the hopes of a continent

Delicately balanced on their heads.

Not a Night of Sleep

This city doesn't sleep,

Its music will keep you awake

The sirens will wail in your dreams,

Its cars will honk until the morning comes.

The curtains illuminated in flashes of reds and blues,

Keeping the emergency personnel on their toes,

The gunshots no longer frightening

And the screams in the shadows when a woman is knifed or robbed,

Have all become part of the stars,

Part of the night.

Every morning I had to count

The heads of my family and friends

And pray that no one is missing.

AZANIA, The Fading Rainbow

The rainbow that held

The storms away is fading to smoke

And now dark clouds gather

To cast the beloved land in shadows.

It's in these shadows where gunshots are issued;

A woman screams or a corpse lain in silence.

It's in these shadows where the youth trot barefoot

Back and forth, jobless and hungry;

Hoping, searching the horizons

For a new kind of a rainbow.

African Baobabs

From the sudden swelling of the earth
Pregnant with seedlings,
They heave out of the sand
And shoot out of the dry land,
Unfolding and unfurling
Like parachutes in a windless sky.

Sprouting and growing
They branch out like arms
Of a Vitruvian man,
With gigantic roots creating
A home in a waterless world
Where they'll grow imposing
Against the sky,
Against the hills,
Against the mountains
To become landmarks of hope and resilience.

In seasons of floods, fires and storms;

These giants of greenery

Will stand unshaken to the horizons

And keep rooted to the land

As they learn to grow back

From wounds of saws and axes

Knowing that they'll live yet again

In this changing and uncertain world.

The Drunkard

A drunken man

Saunters with confidence

And a bit of singing

Into a squalid looking home,

He finds children mired in mud

And dirt

Playing

Hide and seek in the yard.

He asks" where is your father?"

A steel faced woman

Comes out of the house,

Picks a stone

And shoves the drunkard out of the yard

Then hit him hard at his back

And she asks, "do you know us?"

The drunkard run away

Clutching at his painful spine

And wondering if he entered a wrong house.

House Chores

She hums her songs as she goes,

Reassuring melodies that echoes

In the kitchen and trails her back

And forth as she moves

Around the house,

Around the yard,

Shaking her elegant figure

And swinging her hips;

Her apron drenched by water

And stained with flour

Flutter in the wind like a flag

Swaying victoriously as she comes

Bearing bowls full of food

To feed a famished family.

Laughter and Cries

The child begins to cry

Mother gives her

A breast full of milk

She sucks and fills

Her tiny stomach

Mother gently touches

And tugs playfully at

Her chubby cheeks

They both break

In a fit of giggles

Mother and child

Dead in laughter.

Cleaning Services

Outside the window,

A rubber rake scrapes

The ground,

The spade chips and churn

The soil,

Cutting away the grass

Clearing yesterday's

Footprints on the walkway,

Leaves and twigs

All gathered and burnt,

To create a new canvas

Awaiting new memories -

New footsteps

Coming or leaving

A place that resembles home

The First Raindrop

So high above you come

In a steep downward dive,

Falling through spacious a dome,

So long your travels until you arrive.

Whether you fall or fly

Tanks and buckets all ready,

All dams, rivers and reservoirs

Remain agape unto the sky.

The earth shakes and trembles

As you crushed in the desert,

Sending millions and millions

Of scattering droplets across the fields.

When you begin your fall,

There were moments between your drops

Where I used to pause and count to ten and beyond

Before the next drop on our rooftops.

But then you'll begin to race
And whip our houses with angry tides,
Uprooting trees and walls
And I couldn't keep up with your pace.

The lightning would strike our cries,
Cars and houses swept off their feet
And we watched on as our loved ones died
Before the arrival of humanitarian fleet.

Nowadays rains kill people!
Times have changed, so is the world;
Our greed, our negligence, our plastics,
Our oil, our mining has changed the world.

Where Do You Come From

You see;

Those ruins there!

That roofless RDP house

With a faded plaster,

Yes! The one with cracks on the walls

And ghostly footsteps tormenting

The hallways.

The one that trembles and

Stagger when a little wind

Blows.

That with a door

Kicked ajar

And broken windows,

There! Where masked men

Came in one night

And stole the furniture.

Those crumbling walls

Up on that ravaged land I can't call my own,

There, my friend! Is home.

Mob Justice

He swiftly snatched the bag,

Flung through the crowd-

Poor GoGo screamed and chased the thug,

A commotion ensued, with varied alarms too loud.

He shoved and forced his way out,

Someone seized him by the belt-

When he turned and faced around,

He was bleeding, pain he suddenly felt.

If you ever saw ants upon a wriggling worm

The scene wouldn't have you surprised,

The fellow never knew how to escape the storm;

But silently prayed to Lord Christ.

He was dealt with punches and kicks,

Twisted this way and that-

Pelted with clubs and bricks

And swam in his own blood.

When the mob quenched its thirst for blood
The bag was restored to the poor GoGo,
They watched the boy bleeding where he lay
Until God intervened, the spirit left the body.

The Demonstrators

A mob of disgruntled citizens

Marched in their dozens,

Picketed and chanted for so long

Singing a liberation song.

Then came the police

From no official office,

The crowd began to run

After the deployment of a gun.

The multitudes stirred in motion

Terrified voices began to yell

As some stumbled and fell

Amidst the chaos and confusion.

And death became their freedom

A warning never to march against this kingdom.

My Midnight Star

Mighty midnight star
You distinguish yourself
Amongst millions of stars,
Shine the brightest of them all,
Let your brightness
Shine upon my face,
Mighty midnight star
Let your sparkle
Bring happiness to my heart,
Let your light
Bring freedom to my soul,
Mighty midnight star
I wish you could shine forever
For I will forever look upon you.

Home Sparrows

When the kitchen door is left open
The sparrows fly in and dine on the table,
Picking crumbs with their tiny beaks
And their eyes gloss glistening like marble.

They flutter with little wings past my head,
Scurry outside to perch upon a tree
In surveillance of another opportunity
When the door is left open and unattended.

Their chatter on the trees is harmonious,
Melodious melodies makes it home
And fill the skies with their music,
A place we may all call home.

But there are times when it could be silent,
When sparrows have flown away
And we would wonder for a moment

If they would return home to dine with us yet again.

Death

It might dine with me today

And untimely take me away,

Uninvited it might knock

On your door tomorrow

And arrive unannounced

In your living room,

A guest we all have to meet

Yet its arrival unwelcome,

We might live our lives justly

Helping others or extravagantly

Without any care in the world

Yet its treatment is always the same,

Young and old hearts

Are dealt with equal harshness,

We only take hope in that it might relieve us

Of our current burdens

And take us to a better space,

A green and colourful place

Where we wish for joy and happiness

And hope we never have to meet

Its darkness again.

Household Accountant

Every month end

When the government grant

Has been paid out to her,

She sits by the table;

Thoughtful and in contemplation

Of what to write

On her grocery list,

Even though the money

Was not enough

To cover all the necessities

Of our huge household –

It's still a miracle to this day

How mother managed

To take care of us all.

Smoking Guns

The lamentation of their screams

Floated homeward upon the waves

And sailed back across the seas

To be anchored in our troubled hearts.

The sound of the gun shots

Became a beating drum,

An anthem children had to learn

Before they could learn to live.

Somehow the wailing moon

Raised tides in our eyes,

Only to draw back and leave us in loss

Before we saw phantom ships returning.

Whip scarred and handcuffed,

Mounts of their corpses scatter

And grow on the hard sidewalks

Like bleeding wild mushrooms.

If only the world could pause
Somewhere in dawn or dusk
And let a new day begin,
Begin and end this cold war.

Painting

So dark the world can be

When in the hallways we walk

To a place we can't see

And voices in our heads talk.

We paint our houses

With lighter colours

That douses

This dark shaded hearts of ours.

We paint a picture

Depicting our history

And wonders of nature

While telling tales of our story.

Paint lightens our lives,

It gives taste to our buildings

So that they may survive

A tough and harsh world.

When It's Dark

When it's silent and dark
Under the African stars you sat,
When all dogs seized to bark
Under the tree you spot a cat.

When stars begin to fall
And shadows begin to creep
Squeeze yourself against a wall
And try not to weep.

Nature's hazards abounds,
We live in a world of horrors,
Horrible smells, sights and sounds
Mingling into a terrifying chorus.

But dear please don't run
Soon you shall see the sun.

Listening to music

Every Sunday afternoon

I sit on the front stoep and listen to music.

Speakers blaring out a booming bass and beat

Within which I hear a note coming, from a distant.

I hear it somewhere between

The silences of the instruments

And anticipate its melodious arrival.

I listen within the matrix of the music

For the sound of a door opening

To an enchanting harmonious timbre.

To fill and deluge the spaces of this silence

With chorus and rhythm

Such I've never heard before.

Then suddenly, like rain –

The song is brought to an abrupt end,

Quietude and silence fills the sky.

A musical note is left in the air

And in my heart too,

Tempting my old bones into dancing.

The Black Crow

There is something

About a black Crow,

That has to do with the undertaking

Of living souls,

Not that I'm superstitious

But the way in which

It clasps its wings

Behind its back

And walks like death

Around living beings.

Its eyes a deep blackness,

A window connecting

The past and the future,

Forgotten memories

And tomorrow's uncertainties

Conquering Fear

It was on days like these
When I would beg the earth to unfold
And swallow me whole,
When I hid behind a stalk of grass flailing in the wind
To keep myself invisible.

When fear walked the corridors of my heart
Like a warden with a baton
Every time I tried to raise my head.

Fear was a tyrant tied me captive,
My body a cocoon without apertures
For escape.

Then like a butterfly, I felt myself
Outgrowing my chains,
Wings pushing against walls –
A twinkling light through the gabs.

I shoved out and flew skyward

Broke into the beautiful sunlight

And the world welcomed me in a song,

Higher and higher I took my flight.

Rain

I lay in silence and listened;
Listened to the coming of rain,
Tentative at first, one drop after another
Upon a corrugated roofing.

Then it would suddenly stop,
Rain and I, listened to each other,
A moment of silence before another drop
And another one there after.

Unpredictable, it would begin to race, to rave
And rush, drumming down upon the roof
In torrents and echoes so loud that
It will sound like an angry river.

It will whip and lash at the windows,
At the walls, at the doors and stop.
Another silence and I listened again

And heard sparrows chirping on the trees.

Whirlwinds of Freedom

Fear not the coming storm;
Sometimes you are like a plastic
Rustling in the wind,
Caught fluttering upon a razor fence
Seeking to take to the sky.
Wire spikes tearing at your skin –
Holding you fast,
Leaving you in scars and shreds
Until you tear in half,
One half would take to the skies
And the other
Left struggling still –
Wait for another whirlwind
To set it free.

THABANG (REJOICE)

She slipped and fell

Spilling her waters like a calabash

Upon the polished floor,

We tried calling the ambulance

But there was no signal,

A boy was called across the street

To run as fast as possible –

On legs adhered with dust

To summon Naledi; the midwife –

Who lived on the other side of the valley.

Spilt waters can't be recouped.

Naledi gathered the girl together

With skilled hands,

She probed

Caressed

And pressed with tenderness

Until amidst the moans and sweat
A child's cry broke into the silence
Of worried faces,

The child's cry became a joyous song
Welcomed
With ululations by the once terrified
Faces,
The girl named her child "THABANG".

Lost In Love

I've lost my many things,

Memories of friends,

Hats, jackets and cell phones –

But your love

Still clings on the edges of an empty hole

In my heart

And refuse to get lost.

After all these years,

After all these changes,

When I look at you,

I see a lifetime of sunshine

Going back to reignite

The gloom all of my dark days.

Then when I thought to be wrong,

I see it in your eyes, on your smile,

A bright face like a million sunflowers,

I recognise the love I wished to find
In other people's faces.

Then I'm content to get lost
In the galaxies of your eyes,
And live in there forever.

Your Touch

Your touch is my torch in this darkness,

You lit up my world when I was uprooted

From zones of comfort and became a flash

Of warmth and hope to my weakening self,

Your touch; unforgettable, a signature etched

On my beating heart where it shall remain

Forever after I have ceased to be, then peacefully

I will recline beneath the grass

Upon which another paradise shall be built.

Searching for Love?

Have you been searching for love?
Emptied all the buckets
And scrutinized your trouser pockets,
Even though you knew it isn't there?

Have you been searching for love,
In a hidden corner or a dark place?
Maybe you might have found it
In the mirror that reflects your face.

Maybe if you have searched
In your heart or in your soul,
You might have known where it always was;
In the flesh that make up your whole being.

I'm Human

I'm human,

I wear my skin

Upon my bones

To cover my soul.

I'm human,

I grow ideas in my head

Nourishing my imagination

To recreate the world.

I'm human,

I learn from my past

The history of humanity

To take me a step further.

I'm human,

I touch tenderly

The hearts of my dearest

To cherish our love.

I'm human,
Wingless, yet always in flight
To direct my soul
Upon the path of universal light.

Who Are We?

We begin at the end

When the story is told

The last sentence written,

We begin curled small as a full stop.

We grow to be puzzled by the world

Astonished at how quickly we grow tall

And walk around

Like an exclamation mark!

At the end of a history told

And long forgotten.

Our backs will be curved and crooked

Stooping like a question mark

Upon a walking stick,

As we grow tired and grey haired

Wondering if is it too late to be asking;

"Who are we?".

Home, A Battlefield

One dark afternoon

Thabo comes home from school,

Opens his backpack

Takes out a whole lump of a poem

And puts it on the kitchen table

"Mama, Ma'm Tladi gave us homework"

And she says: "damn it Thabo, there's no

Place for a poem on the kitchen table, go

Show it to your father,

He sleeps in the guestroom!"

Behind Closed Doors

They disappeared
Behind Closed doors
And left me in the silence
Of a world stricken by a pandemic,
Oh! How dark a moment that was.

They spied at me
Through curtained windows
And half opened doors
Like cats after rain
Afraid of the mud.

Life paused
And stood still for months,
I tip-toed
Across the deserted town
Somewhere in 2019
When the streets were thrown into

Loneliness.

I met a man or two

With gloved hands

And masked faces

Struggling

To keep away their tears,

On a Sunday morning, a good morning

For a funeral.

No school children

Ran through the playing fields,

No church choirs

Sung praises on Sunday,

Women, men and children

All whispered;

Go away,

COVID.

Go away,

Won't you stop killing us?

A Home of Storms

When my father comes home –
He comes as a sack of nails,
Of broken bottles and other spiked things

He arrives to empty himself in the house
And I would shut myself up in my room,
Listening to mother limping and tiptoeing

Around words as sharp as swords,
Sometimes she pours tears on the rock
That is my father, thinking he would soften up,

But his voice seeps in underneath the door
To test and stab at my bleeding heart,
I stick headphones to my ears

And turn up the volume to Hillsong praises;
Wondering how can I praise the Lord

When He is not here with me, to calm the storms.

Love Will Find You

Yes, it will come –
It will come when you least expect it,
When you sit by yourself watching
The river flow tranquil before you,
Or when you sit on the bench
In a public park watching the pigeons
Scrambling for crumbs.

A hand will touch your shoulder from
Behind,
Envelope you in its warmth –
Yes, there it shall find you and you will rise
To take its hand and walk away,
To where the river comes tumbling from;
The very origin of tranquillity.

I'm the Colour of the Night

I'm the colour of the night
With glistening and sparkling falling stars.

I'm the colour of the night
With fireflies swirling on the grass.

I'm the colour of the night
With a floating moon across dark skies.

I'm the colour of the night
With crickets singing on the grass.

I'm the colour of the night
With candle light on a distant hill.

I'm the colour of the night
Before the morning could arrive.

A Beautiful Sight

I've never seen a beautiful sight in my life,
In all I've seen and places I've been
Whether in happy times or times of strife,
A sight so phenomenal and lean.

Much had been said and I've heard much,
Men and women tell tales of beauty,
But I've never seen a sight as such,
So magical, magnificent and full of beauty.

A sight so natural as the glistening stones
Of ancient Kilimanjaro, somehow coming alive,
Enchanting, like a remedy that atones
One's feelings, I've never believed my eyes could be this alive.

That what I see; a human torso marked
By hills and caverns rival to that of earth, naked.

Dust to Dust

Then we ask who my come to save

Souls perpetually pulled by gravity

Into the deep depravity

Of the damned darkened grave.

We fear the coming of death

That has never been early nor late,

The grass await to embrace us

And finally adorn us with earth.

We are summoned to the unknown

And carried out upon invisible wings

To meet our celestial kings

Whom none, my dispute, their crown.

It is in this damned dark mount of a dome

That I shall gladly and eternally call home.

The Naked Night of the City

When the city slump to sleep, another rises
Up in its wake
Like a tide rising to the moon,
Laid bare under the stars and fluorescent
Lights,
Taxi's ferry workers back to their dwellings
Like a convoy of ants from a kitchen table
Crawling upon the wall with crumbs carried,
In moments the city is deserted
The night opens its doors for darkness,
Music drift down from a third floor nightclub,

Where a woman descend down the stairs,
She lift her skirt and bends to a dark figure
Stooping over her-
Another vagrant vagabond veers into the street
Turning the trash bins upside down
Before he drowns a warm cola down his throat

And throws the empty bottle on the pavement,

A drunkard in dirty tattered trousers
Strike a conversation with a fashion doll
That stood posing adorned in suit and bowtie
On the other side of the world, beyond the display glass,
Ignored; he mumbled and tumbled
On his way to God knows where.

Across the squalid city square
A boy turns a corner,
Pushing a trolley laden with refuse bags
Filled full with plastic bottles,
Ignorantly saving the planet
And intently trying to survive
A jungle swamped with predators.

One of which crouch at a corner
Waiting patiently like a cat at the door
Of a mouse's hole, ready to pounce on late stragglers,

Before the screams are heard in the shadows.

The night sky fills with sirens and chiming alarms,

Blue and red lights illuminate the street like a Christmas Tree,

Police arrive like father Christmas ran out of gifts to give

For free,

Shabby men are shoved into a police van,

Both the guilty and the innocent

Will spend a night in custody.

At dawn figures shrink back to shadows,

Humanity wakes from its comfortable pillows,

Newspaper headlines grab their attention;

"A woman killed last night."

"Two men arrested for mugging and robbery."

"A suspected rapist at large."

"A girl missing still not found."

Then the city fills itself up again, it's a new day,

New merchandise for another night

For another life to disappear in the shadows.

Home is a Box

I have tried to gather this poem
Into a wooden box,
Words, metaphors and non-existent rhyme
But it slipped through my fingers
Like a fish,
Grew wings like a pigeon
And flew away.

But then
I kept the box open,
Filled it with water
For fish can't stay long on dry sand
And even a pigeon
Needs drink once in a while,
So I waited, for a homing pigeon.

Hide and Seek

"The rooster,

The rooster,

It calls "

She says with eyes closed

"Eggs" Comes a reply

Somewhere in a hidden corner

"How many?"

She asks still with eyes closed

"Twenty" comes another reply from

Behind the fire hut

"One, two, three…"

She counts up to twenty

"May I come?"

"Yes" says a voice underneath

The old broken tractor

"It comes, ready or not"

She runs to the wreckage of the tractor

And finds Themba crouching

Upon the grease

"I found you"

She says and runs back,

Only to find Sarah clocking upon the wall

And shouting;

"Home safe,

Home safe"

But Isabella, never came home that day.

She was never found again.

The Wardrobe

The wardrobe you have bequeathed to me
Has fallen from the bricks
And leans heavily against the wall.

Termites had gnawed its door
And dislodged it from the hinges
Until it can't close anymore.

They have carried the mahogany splinters
In heaps of rubble
And gathered them to the corner
So thick and remote
Where my broom can't reach.

Rats had bitten at the hem of the apron
You left hanging from the rail,
The ID in its pocket had crumbled
And smudged at the corners;

In which you are still declared Deceased,

In an ink stamp still dark and wet

As if you left us yesterday.

The Curfew

Now and then

I remember those days;

If you take back the years

That I have floated forth

Buoyant upon my tears

You'll meet me in my youth

Standing in front of a hut

Fingers stuffed in my mouth

Tears stuck in my eyes

Naked and barefoot

Watching a yellow police van

Pass by my granny's courtyard

Before she grabbed me inside

And fastened the door shut.

Sky Blue

I swear

I saw a face

Across the surface of the moon,

Clouds floated like a landscape

Where I fear

I might have seen bodies laying about,

A scene of ancient battlefield

Descending down to earth,

Then came the wind like a broom

To sweep the floor of the sky, blue.

0091 The Train To Mamelodi

Can I still buy tomatoes
On the nine one train that rides
From Mamelodi to the city?
Five rands a packet they used to be
And fat, fresh tomatoes at that.

Can I still buy apples
On the nine one train that rides
From the township to the city?
Five rands a packet they used to be
And fat, fresh apples at that.

Can I still ride in the nine one
That comes down from Pretoria
With commuters hanging upon it,
Like a worm accosted by ants
Slowly wriggling its way to Mamelodi?

Can I still attend the sermon

In carriage three where passengers sing,

Praying for the nine one to reach town,

Praying for the nine one to sell tomatoes

And apples at five rands a packet.

The Calling

Your ancestors call upon you

To become a healer.

The bones point to a river

Mami Wata calls from the caverns

Of subterranean lakes,

Where her castle floats in all its grandeur,

Seeking to teach you secrets of the deep:

How to see with eyes closed

Like a blind Cyclops,

How to banish death from bodies so young

Inflicted by unimaginable maladies.

Go on your chosen path,

There's no "No" for an answer.

Your ancestors call upon you

To become a healer.

Afloat

I enter a room

Furnished with grief and gloom

And empty out my pockets

On the bed,

Search and sift through everything;

Coins, confusion and entanglements

Of the life I have lived,

I pick up the year which I have been

The most happy

And go to bed holding on to it

As I remain afloat upon my tears,

Drifting to a sunny shore.

Tears Fall Away From Home

Hammid left Sudan three years ago
Opened a tuck shop in South Africa
His father died in the first war
His brothers and sisters too

Yesterday, I went to buy bread at his shop
And found him broken and crying
It took a while to get him talking
Before he told me his mother was dead

Now, his tears fall in another country
Far away from home
"Men don't cry" I try to console him
I take my bread and go home

I can't go on drinking the tea
I turn my face up east and listen to the wind
I swear I might have heard sounds of gunshots

Across the African sky.

The Entire Lifetime Of A Poem

I'm here

Said the poem

Announcing its arrival

As it enters

Young and fresh

And like all new things

A minute more

It grows old

And like all old things

Through the door

It leaves.

Red Sunset

One beautiful African morning
The militia came down to town
In Jeeps with machine guns,
Like famers during the harvest season
And began reaping and slaughtering
Lives out of innocent civilians,
Cutting down hopes and dreams
Of children of the black cradle
Like sickle through the grass;
That day the sun went down red with blood,
And a seed of hatred implanted
In the hearts of children
Born out of one womb.

Would You Love Me?

Would you love me

If I dropped three hearts

On your story, painted them red

And left a blushing emoji?

Would you come running

If I dropped my location in your DM

And promised you paradise

Beyond the screen in your hand?

Would you accept me

With all my faults and toothless gums,

Smiling and beaming at you

On our first meet up?

Or will you run away

So I would never see you again?

Moon Watch

When watching the wearied moon

Wrecked and blasted by asteroids and

Blazing boulders out of space

It draws me near its dormant drab

Of a surface suffused with scattered

Matter and metrics of lunar rocks

I'm drawn deeper into the mysteries

Of a momentous space, a sky sparsely

Seized by sparkling stars

My gaze follow the gallant fall

Of an earthbound star

Only to disappear behind silhouettes of trees

Closer within touch, closer within reach

A dark sky extends its hand to caress

Faces upturned skyward, all watching.

It Will Be Okay

In the silence of a winter night
I tug myself into cold sheets,
Into a bed furnished with grief-
Tears spilling on the pillows.

I slept on with a wearied heart
Curled up like an Okapi knife-
Beside me, an empty space
A body's outline of a loved one.

There are no more cosy night cuddles
To cut the silence of the cold night,
Then I would open my heart
Like a shed of tools,

Looking for something like "sorry"
Or "it will be okay", but my thoughts uncinch
Like an old family photo album

Memories nudging me to smile again.

A Bright Face, A Guiding Light

Have you seen her face

Appear in the sky,

Saw it fade and erode away

And you wanted to cry?

Then a handkerchief offered

By a hand, trembling –

The world all dark,

The sun behind the clouds, waiting.

Everything rise;

Your emotions, your tears,

A body from the chair – the rain rise

Upward and summer comes from below.

The sky return itself to blue

Your grandmother's face reveal its rays

From behind the clouds

As the sun in your troubled days.

Down And Out

There was a particular year

When I had nothing to wear

And nobody wanted me near,

When I talked nobody wanted to hear –

Even those I held dear

Turned their backs on me and showed me their rear

Because I was down

At the bottom of the bottomless,

The entire town

Lost hope in me because I was homeless

And had nothing to own.

Then when I tried

They said it was the last kick of a dying horse

Little did they know

It was the first kick of a waking horse.

Clenching Jaws

There is no
Kinder way
To chew
A bone,

It has to do
With the
Clenching
Of jaws.

I Wish I'd Said

I wish I'd said "I love you"
Before the clocks ran late
And honoured my due

I wish I'd paid my respects
Before you met your fate
Where crossroads intersects

I wish I'd said my goodbyes
Before you closed the gate
That opens when the living dies

I wish I'd said farewell my friend
My companion, my mate
We all have to arrive at the end.

Slain

I still hear echoes of your voice
In the silence of the hallways,
Angry and against the choices
I've made, every time and always.

The cracks on the glass stir memories,
Thoughts plunge back to that miserable day
When your rage and all your worries
Erupted like mount Vesuvius,

Smashing every little thing on its way
The window is still patched with cardboard,
There are words I can't say –
The smoke still smell fresh in my nose.

There is still a hole on the kitchen door
Where you have kicked it in
And I still feel the coldness of the floor

Where you have left me slain.

Wayfinding

Anyway, I feel like
I have been here before,

But where else would you go
When you are halfway
In the middle of too late?

Born In Chaos

We are born

In the assemblage

Of smouldering

Fire and ice.

We are growing

In the whirlpool

Of exploding mountains

And crashing stars.

But still something

Hold us in place,

Upright to journey alongside

A ray of light.

The Christmas Of Old

When Christmas was still Christmas
We would wait in anticipation
Near the front door –
Which we rarely opened
Unless we had guests of high import!

When the festive days draws near
We would cheer at the passing cars
Where cars seldom pass by.

We would wake up in the middle of the night
When headlights illuminates
The window panes
And expect to hear a knock on the door.

Our guests are no ordinary visitors
This are family members whose faces
Cling to a thin string

Over cliffs of our childhood memories,

And they come bearing

All manner of sweetmeats.

Sometimes a once clean chin, may return

Bearing a cluster of a beard,

Or a smooth skin return

Tattooed by scars of age.

In rooms that were once silent

And dark throughout the year,

Beds that are never slept in –

Beds that are permanently made

Would now stir themselves back to life

To be occupied once again

By laughter, chatter and merriment

Of our nostalgic past.

When Christmas was still Christmas

We would run along the streets,

Clad in our new clothing

And cheap Chinese shoes.

We didn't care much for designer labels

As long as they came new from the box.

Only yesterday did we realise

That Christmas was just another day.

Mmap New African Poets Series

If you have enjoyed *Mother's Kitchen and Other Places*, consider these other fine books in the **New African Poets Series** from *Mwanaka Media and Publishing:*

I Threw a Star in a Wine Glass by Fethi Sassi
Best New African Poets 2017 Anthology by Tendai R Mwanaka and Daniel Da Purificacao
Logbook Written by a Drifter by Tendai Rinos Mwanaka
Mad Bob Republic: Bloodlines, Bile and a Crying Child by Tendai Rinos Mwanaka
Zimbolicious Poetry Vol 1 by Tendai R Mwanaka and Edward Dzonze
Zimbolicious Poetry Vol 2 by Tendai R Mwanaka and Edward Dzonze
Zimbolicious: An Anthology of Zimbabwean Literature and Arts, Vol 3 by Tendai Mwanaka
Under The Steel Yoke by Jabulani Mzinyathi
Fly in a Beehive by Thato Tshukudu
Bounding for Light by Richard Mbuthia
Sentiments by Jackson Matimba
Best New African Poets 2018 Anthology by Tendai R Mwanaka and Nsah Mala
Words That Matter by Gerry Sikazwe
The Ungendered by Delia Watterson
Ghetto Symphony by Mandla Mavolwane
Sky for a Foreign Bird by Fethi Sassi
A Portrait of Defiance by Tendai Rinos Mwanaka
Zimbolicious: An Anthology of Zimbabwean Literature and Arts, Vol 4 by Tendai Mwanaka and Jabulani Mzinyathi
When Escape Becomes the only Lover by Tendai R Mwanaka
وَيَسهَرُ اللَّيلُ عَلَى شَفَتِي...وَالغَمَام by Fethi Sassi
A Letter to the President by Mbizo Chirasha
This is not a poem by Richard Inya

Pressed flowers by John Eppel
Righteous Indignation by Jabulani Mzinyathi:
Blooming Cactus by Mikateko Mbambo
Rhythm of Life by Olivia Ngozi Osouha
Travellers Gather Dust and Lust by Gabriel Awuah Mainoo
Chitungwiza Mushamukuru: An Anthology from Zimbabwe's Biggest Ghetto Town by Tendai Rinos Mwanaka
Zimbolicious: An Anthology of Zimbabwean Literature and Arts, Vol 5 by Tendai Mwanaka
Because Sadness is Beautiful? by Tanaka Chidora
Of Fresh Bloom and Smoke by Abigail George
Shades of Black by Edward Dzonze
Best New African Poets 2020 Anthology by Tendai Rinos Mwanaka, Lorna Telma Zita and Balddine Moussa
This Body is an Empty Vessel by Beaton Galafa
Between Places by Tendai Rinos Mwanaka
Best New African Poets 2021 Anthology by Tendai Rinos Mwanaka, Lorna Telma Zita and Balddine Moussa
Zimbolicious: An Anthology of Zimbabwean Literature and Arts, Vol 6 by Tendai Mwanaka and Chenjerai Mhondera
A Matter of Inclusion by Chad Norman
Keeping the Sun Secret by Mariel Awendit
سِجلٌّ مَكْتُوبٌ لِثَائِهِ by Tendai Rinos Mwanaka
Ghetto Blues by Tendai Rinos Mwanaka
Zimbolicious: An Anthology of Zimbabwean Literature and Arts, Vol 7 by Tendai Rinos Mwanaka and Tanaka Chidora
Best New African Poets 2022 Anthology by Tendai Rinos Mwanaka and Helder Simbad
Dark Lines of History by Sithembele Isaac Xhegwana
a sky is falling by Nica Cornell
Death of a Statue by Samuel Chuma
Along the way by Jabulani Mzinyathi
Strides of Hope by Tawanda Chigavazira

Young Galaxies by Abigail George
Coming of Age by Gift Sakirai

Soon to be released

https://facebook.com/MwanakaMediaAndPublishing/

www.ingramcontent.com/pod-product-compliance
Lightning Source LLC
Chambersburg PA
CBHW070310230426
43664CB00015B/2709